This book belongs to:

_____

AND I DON'T GIVE A FUCK!

© Maz Scales 2019

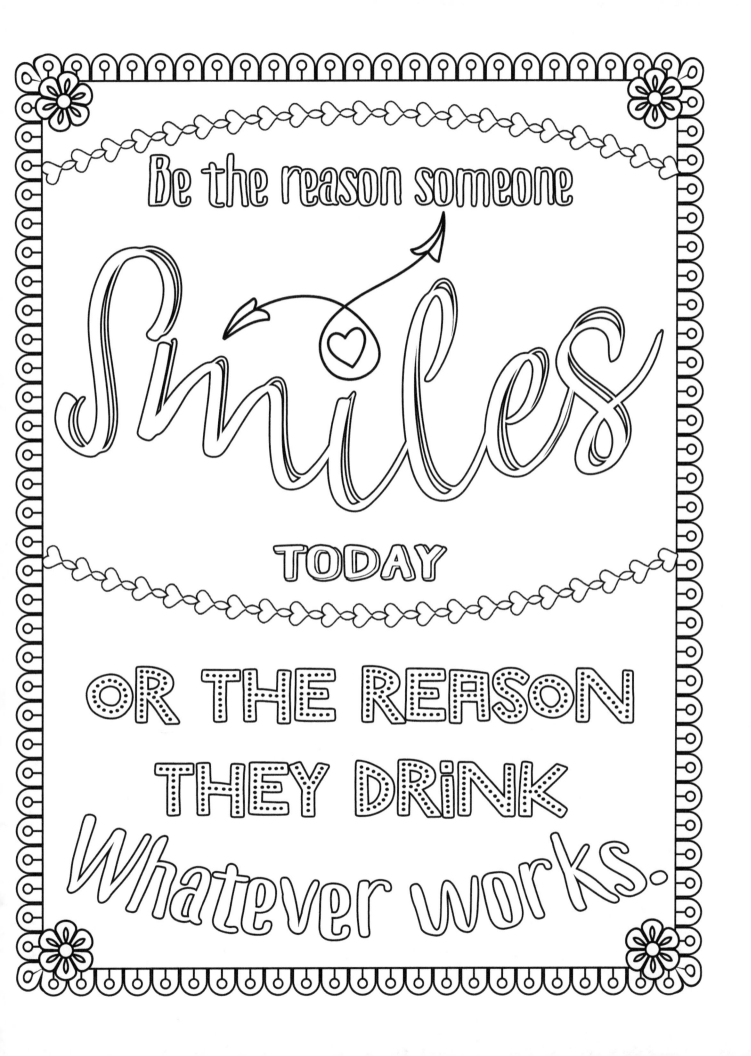

So FUCK This Shit!

There's no more to color!

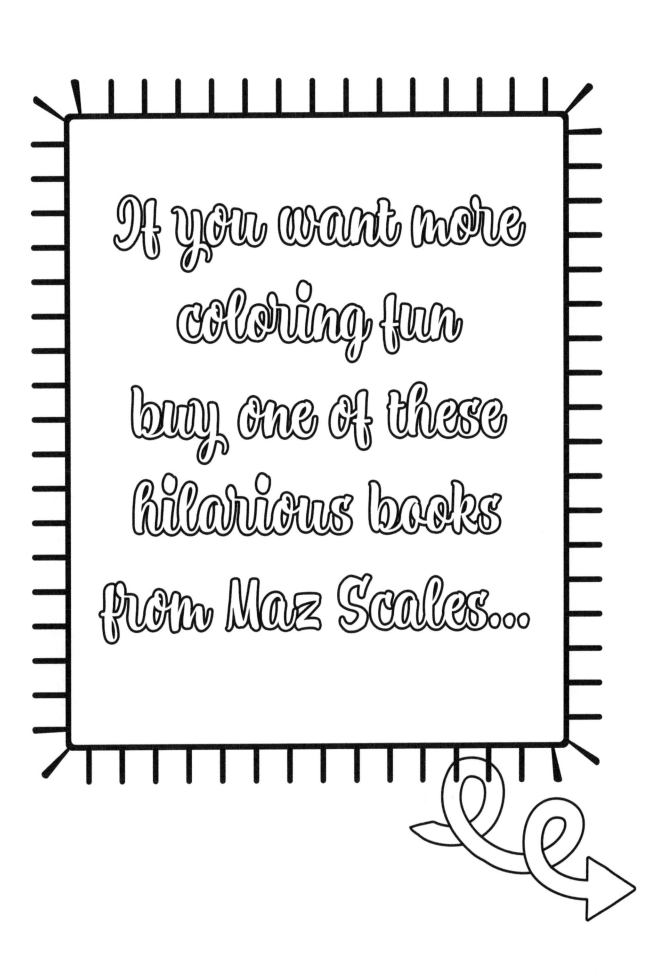

UNICORNS FARTING COLORING BOOKS

A Hilarious Look At The Secret Life of The Unicorn.

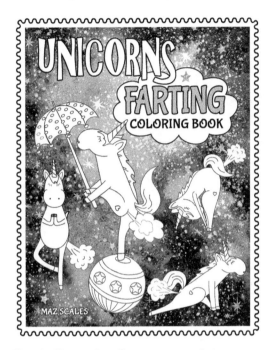

Get Book One on Amazon:
http://bit.ly/fartsbook1

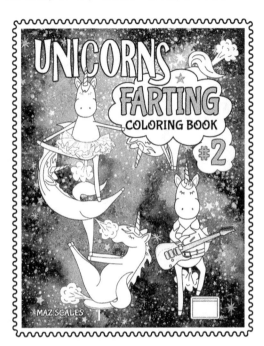

Get Book Two on Amazon:
http://bit.ly/fartsbook2

Get Book Three on Amazon:
http://bit.ly/fartsbook3

Unicorns are special and magical creatures.
They are beautiful, majestic and pure.
They carry themselves with dignity and pride wherever they go.
But, they have a secret unknown to most........
they love to FART!

They break wind anywhere and everywhere.
They really love to share their odious explosions.
So if you smell something noxious in the air
and you don't know where it came from,
there is probably a Unicorn close by,
etting one rip.
Now anytime you drop one at an
inappropriate time, just blame a Unicorn!

Fun Gift Idea For Silly People of All Ages.

Here are a couple of sample pages from my Unicorns Farting Coloring Book.
Enjoy!

COLOR TESTING PAGE

COLOR TESTING PAGE

COLOR TESTING PAGE

www.ingramcontent.com/pod-product-compliance
Lightning Source LLC
LaVergne TN
LVHW071528301224
800237LV00023B/820